My book of
playtime
rhymes

Illustrated by MARGARET CHAMBERLAIN

Ladybird Books

Boys and girls, come out to play,
The moon does shine as bright as day.
Leave your supper, and leave your sleep,
Come to your playfellows in the street.
Come with a whoop, come with a call,
Come with a good will, or not at all.
Up the ladder and down the wall,
A halfpenny loaf will serve us all.
You find milk and I'll find flour,
And we'll have a pudding in half an hour.

Georgie Porgie, pudding and pie,
Kissed the girls and made them cry.
When the boys came out to play,
Georgie Porgie ran away.

See-saw, Margery Daw,
Johnny shall have a new master.
He shall have but a penny a day,
Because he can't work any faster.

Here we go round the mulberry bush,
The mulberry bush, the mulberry bush,
Here we go round the mulberry bush,
On a cold and frosty morning.

Ring-a-ring o' roses,
A pocket full of posies;
A-tishoo! A-tishoo!
We all fall down.

Pat-a-cake, pat-a-cake, baker's man,
Bake me a cake as fast as you can!
Roll it and pat it and mark it with "B,"
And put it in the oven for baby and me.

Dance to your daddy, my bonnie laddie;
Dance to your daddy, my bonnie lamb.
You shall have a fishy on a little dishy,
You shall have a fishy when the boat comes in.

Ride, baby, ride,
Pretty baby shall ride,
And have a little puppy dog tied to her side,
And a little pussy cat tied to the other,
And away she shall ride to see her grandmother.

I love little Pussy,
  Her coat is so warm,
And if I don't hurt her
  She'll do me no harm.
So I'll not pull her tail,
  Nor drive her away,
But Pussy and I
  Very gently will play.

Polly, put the kettle on,
Polly, put the kettle on,
Polly, put the kettle on,
We'll all have tea.

Sukey, take it off again,
Sukey, take it off again,
Sukey, take it off again,
They've all gone away.

Rain, rain, go away,
Come again another day;
Little Tommy wants to play.

One, two, buckle my shoe;
Three, four, knock at the door;

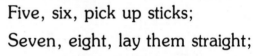

Five, six, pick up sticks;
Seven, eight, lay them straight;

Nine, ten, a big fat hen;
Eleven, twelve, dig and delve;

Thirteen, fourteen, maids are courting;
Fifteen, sixteen, maids in the kitchen;

Seventeen, eighteen, maids are waiting;
Nineteen, twenty, my plate's empty.

My mother said that I never should
Play with the gypsies in the wood.
If I did, she would say,
"Naughty girl, to disobey."

I had a little castle upon the sand,
One half was water, the other was land.
I opened my little castle door, and guess what I found:
I found a fair lady with a cup in her hand.
The cup was gold, and filled with wine;
Drink, fair lady, and thou shalt be mine!

Ride a cock-horse to Banbury Cross,
    To see a fine lady upon a white horse;
Rings on her fingers and bells on her toes,
    She shall have music wherever she goes.